Suds & Business: A Step by Step Guide to Launching Your Soap Making Business

© Copyright 2023 - All Rights Reserved. The content contained within this book may not be reproduced, duplicated or transmitted without direct written permission from the author or the publisher. Under no circumstances will any blame or legal responsibility be held against the publisher, or author, for any damages, reparation, or monetary loss due to the information contained within this book, either directly or indirectly. Legal Notice: This book is copyright protected. It is only for personal use. You cannot amend, distribute, sell, use, quote or paraphrase any part, or the content within this book, without the consent of the author or publisher. Disclaimer Notice: Please note the information contained within this document is for educational and entertainment purposes only. All effort has been executed to present accurate, up-to-date, reliable, and complete information. No warranties of any kind are declared or implied. Readers acknowledge that the author is not engaged in the rendering of legal, financial, medical or professional advice. The content within this book has been derived from various sources. Please consult a licensed professional before attempting any techniques outlined in this book. By reading this document, the reader agrees that under no circumstances is the author responsible for any losses, direct or indirect, that are incurred as a result of the use of the information contained within this document, including, but not limited to, errors, omissions, or inaccuracies.

Table of Contents

- SOAP MAKING BASICS 10
  - SAFETY FIRST 10
  - PRECISE MEASUREMENTS 10
  - TEMPERATURE MATTERS 11
  - MIXING AND TRACING 11
  - ADDING FRAGRANCE AND COLOR 11
  - LAYERING AND SWIRLING 12
  - MOLDS AND UNMOLDING 12
  - CURING AND PATIENCE 12
  - LABELLING AND RECORD KEEPING 12
  - TROUBLESHOOTING 13
- AN INTRODUCTION TO SOAP MAKING PROCESSES 14
- COLD PROCESS (CP) SOAP MAKING 14
- HOT PROCESS (HP) SOAP MAKING 15
- MELT AND POUR (MP) SOAP MAKING 15
- REBATCHING (HAND-MILLED) SOAP MAKING 15
- LIQUID SOAP MAKING 16
- SWIRL AND LAYER SOAP MAKING 16

TOOLS YOU'LL NEED 17

HOW MUCH INGREDIENTS TO BUY TO BEGIN WITH? 20

SOAP MAKING GLOSSARY 21

INGREDIENTS TO KNOW AND LOVE 26

Base Oils/Fats: 26
Lye (Sodium Hydroxide or Potassium Hydroxide) 27
Additives and Enhancers 27
Superfatting Agents 28
Liquids 29
Hardness and Lathering Enhancers 29
Preservatives: 30
Chelating Agents 30
pH Adjusters 30
Gelling Agents 30

ADDING SCENTS TO YOUR SOAP 31

SOAP RECIPES .... ERROR! BOOKMARK NOT DEFINED.

Luxurious Body Cleansing Bar 34
Repair and Rejuvenate Conditioner Bar 46
Nourish and Hydrate Shampoo Bar .... Error! Bookmark not defined.
Notes .... Error! Bookmark not defined.
Testing Your Soaps 54
Safety First 55

YOUR SOAP MAKING START UP GUIDE 58

Why start a soap making business 58
How much can you earn make selling soaps 60
Where to begin 61
Questions to identify your ideal audience 62
Create a unique selling proposition 63

CRAFTING YOUR IDENTITY: CHOOSING THE PERFECT BUSINESS NAME 64
CRAFTING A SOLID BUSINESS PLAN 66
THE BLUEPRINT FOR SUCCESS: BUILDING A COMPREHENSIVE BUSINESS PLAN .... ERROR! BOOKMARK NOT DEFINED.
DEFINING YOUR MISSION, VISION, AND VALUES 67
MAPPING OUT FINANCIAL PROJECTIONS AND GROWTH STRATEGIES 68
DEVELOP A BUDGET 70
SOURCE YOUR PRODUCT 72
IDENTIFY YOUR SELLING CHANNEL 73
POSITIONING AND BRANDING YOUR SOAP BUSINESS 75
VISUAL IDENTITY MATTERS: DESIGNING A COMPELLING LOGO AND BRAND AESTHETICS 76
SCALING YOUR SOAP BUSINESS .... ERROR! BOOKMARK NOT DEFINED.
FROM SMALL TO BIG: EXPLORING STRATEGIES FOR SCALING YOUR SOAP BUSINESS 77
EXPANDING YOUR PRODUCT LINE: INTRODUCING NEW SOAP VARIATIONS AND RELATED PRODUCTS 78
WHEN TIME IS OF THE ESSENCE: WHOLESALE AND WHITE LABELLING 79
EXPLORING THE WORLD OF WHOLESALE: SELLING YOUR PRODUCTS IN BULK TO RETAILERS 79
WHITE LABELLING: PARTNERING WITH ESTABLISHED BRANDS TO PUT YOUR SOAP CREATIONS ON THE MAP 80
EMBRACING CHALLENGES: ADDRESSING COMMON OBSTACLES AND SETBACKS 81

CELEBRATING VICTORIES: SHOWCASING SUCCESS STORIES FROM FELLOW SOAP MAKING ENTREPRENEURS.........ERROR! BOOKMARK NOT DEFINED.
KNOW THAT YOU KNOW THE BASICS, GET STARTED 82

Introduction

Whether you've been crafting soaps for years or just getting started, there's no better time than now to start a soap making business. With consumers looking for sustainable ways to look after their body, the demand for soaps is high and this trend isn't slowing down. Consumers are more conscious about what they put on their bodies, and they're drawn to the appeal of simple ingredients.

I hope this book will take you on a journey that fuses creativity, science, and business know-how. Whether you're pursuing soap making as a hobby or an aspiring entrepreneur with a dream of building a thriving soap making business, this guide will provide you with the knowledge, inspiration, and practical steps to make your aspirations a reality.

This guide takes you by the hand and walks you through all aspects of launching and growing a soap making business. From developing a solid business plan and branding your unique creations to navigating legal and regulatory requirements, this guide serves as your trusty compass, pointing you towards success in the bustling marketplace.

Soap Making Basics

If you're new to soap making, there are some general rules to keep in mind for the best outcome:

Safety First

As you'll be using ingredients like lye (sodium hydroxide), it's important to ensure safety comes first. This means wearing goggles, gloves, long sleeve shirts and pants and closed toe shoes. Find a workspace that's well ventilated and try to find a space that your pets or children can't access. One handy thing to have is a bottle of vinegar or lemon juice handy to neutralize lye spills.

Precise Measurements

Soap making uses measurements by weight and not by volume. You'll need a digital scale to measure your ingredients accurately. Even slight variations in measurement can impact the quality of your soap.

Temperature Matters

Your formulas will change in temperature as you add and mix your ingredients. You'll need to carefully monitor the temperature of your oils and lye solution. Aim for similar temperatures to prevent graininess and to ensure a smoother mixture.

Mixing and Tracing

Blend your oils and lye mixture thoroughly using a stick blender until you reach "trace". This is the point where the emulsion is stabilized, and where the soap batter thickens and holds its shape.

Adding Fragrance and Color

Incorporate essential oils or fragrance oils at a low trace to ensure they don't evaporate during the saponification process. When using colorants, add them gradually and mix well to achieve your desired hue.

Layering and Swirling

For intricate designs, consider layering different colors of soap batter or using swirling techniques. Practice will improve your skills over time.

Molds and Unmolding

You can use items around the household as your molds but if you're buying new equipment silicone molds are best for easy release and intricate designs. If you choose to use a wooden or cardboard box, you'll want to line it with parchment paper to prevent soap getting stuck.

Curing and Patience

Patience is key when it comes to making soaps that are gentle on the skin. Allow your soap to cure for the recommended time (usually 4-6 weeks) to ensure a milder, longer-lasting bar.

Labelling and Record Keeping

Label your soap with the type, ingredients, and date of production. Keep detailed notes on each batch, including ingredients, measurements, and any adjustments made. This will help you replicate successful batches and troubleshoot issues.

Troubleshooting

Soap making is a craft that takes time to hone. Don't be discouraged if your first batch doesn't look like the ones you see in farmers markets or health food stores. If you'd like to improve your soap making skills, research common soap-making problems and their solutions, such as seizing, overheating, or fragrance fading.

The journey of soap making is a blend of science, art, and personal expression. With dedication, practice, and a willingness to learn, you can create beautiful and unique bars of soap that you'll be proud to share or use yourself.

An Introduction to Soap Making Processes

To understand the basics of soap making, you'll need to be familiar with the most common soap making methods. Here's an overview of each.

Cold Process (CP) Soap Making

This traditional method involves mixing oils and lye (sodium hydroxide) to create a chemical reaction known as saponification. The mixture is poured into molds and left to cure for several weeks, allowing the soap to harden and become milder. Cold process soap making offers endless creative possibilities in terms of color, scent, and design. Many soap makers prefer this method as it holds the integrity of the ingredients more effectively.

Note: Many of the recipes in this book will use the cold process method.

Hot Process (HP) Soap Making

Similar to cold process, hot process soap making involves saponification of oils and lye, but with the added step of applying heat. This speeds up the chemical reaction and results in a soap that can be used almost immediately after curing. The hot process soap making method can give a more rustic appearance and is ideal for those who want to use their soap quickly.

Melt and Pour (MP) Soap Making

Melt and pour is a beginner-friendly method where pre-made soap bases are melted down, and then additives like color, fragrance, and exfoliants are incorporated. The mixture is poured into molds to set. This method is great for creating intricate designs and is perfect for those who are new to soap making. Think of the this method as using a template to make soap.

Rebatching (Hand-Milled) Soap Making

Rebatching involves grating or chopping pre-made soap, melting it, and then adding additional ingredients. This method allows for the incorporation of botanicals, herbs, and essential oils while preserving the benefits of the original soap. Rebatching is a way to create unique soaps with added textures and scents.

Liquid Soap Making

Unlike bar soap, liquid soap is made using potassium hydroxide instead of sodium hydroxide. This method involves a different process and requires more precise measurements. Liquid soap can be used for hand wash, body wash, and even as a base for homemade cleaning products.

Swirl and Layer Soap Making

These techniques can be applied to various soap making methods (cold process, hot process, melt and pour) to create visually striking patterns and designs. Swirling involves layering different colored soap batters and then using a tool to create patterns, while layering involves pouring different colors or scents in distinct layers.

Tools You'll Need

If you're on a budget, you can start your soap making journey with tools you already have in your home. My advice is to make your first batch with things you have around the home and purchase essential equipment to get the job done. Here's a list of key tools you'll need to start making soaps:

Safety goggles: Protect your eyes from potential splashes of lye or other caustic materials.

Gloves: Chemical-resistant gloves shield your hands while working with lye and other ingredients.

Digital scale: Precise measurements of oils, lye, and additives are crucial for a successful batch. As mentioned, slight variations in measurements can affect the outcome of your soaps.

Heat-resistant containers: Containers for measuring and mixing ingredients, such as stainless steel or heat-resistant plastic.

Stick blender: Also known as an immersion blender, it helps blend oils and lye for saponification quickly and thoroughly. It's possible to use a manual whisk but this process will require a lot more time and physical effort.

Candy or digital thermometer: To monitor the temperature of lye solution and oils, ensuring they're within the desired range.

Soap molds: These come in various shapes and sizes for shaping your soap bars. Silicone molds are ideal for intricate designs and easy release of soap after curing. You can also use a cardboard box or shoe box to start with. Be sure to line it with parchment paper to prevent the soap from sticking to your cardboard mold.

Stirring utensils: Stainless steel or silicone spatulas and spoons for mixing ingredients.

Pouring pitchers: Containers with spouts for pouring soap batter into molds.

Work surface: A dedicated area with proper ventilation for soap making.

Plastic table covers or newspapers: To protect surfaces from spills and mess.

Apron: Protect clothing from potential splashes and

Soap cutter: A tool for cleanly cutting and dividing soap bars into uniform sizes.

Curing racks: To allow air circulation and proper curing of soap bars.

Optional Additions:

Essential oils and fragrances: For adding scents to your soap.

Colorants: Such as natural herbs, clays, and micas for creating various colors.

Additives: Botanicals, exfoliants (like oatmeal or coffee grounds), and other ingredients to enhance your soap's texture and properties.
pH testing strips: To ensure the soap has reached the appropriate pH level for safe use.

Remember, different soap-making methods may require additional or specific tools. As you gain experience, you might also explore more specialized equipment to expand your creative possibilities. Prioritize safety and quality by investing in good-quality tools and materials, and always follow proper safety guidelines when working with caustic substances like lye.

How much ingredients should you buy to begin with?

If you're new to soap making and are planning to turn a hobby into a small business, it's best to start small. Buying in bulk may save you money in the short term but you also need to keep in mind that through trial and error you may discover that some ingredients may not suit your soap making process. You may also not have enough time to use the ingredients before they expire. So if you'd like to buy in bulk to save money, opt for buying your base oils in bulk to begin with.

Soap Making Glossary

Saponification: The chemical reaction between oils or fats and an alkali (such as sodium hydroxide or potassium hydroxide) that results in the formation of soap and glycerin.

Lye: An essential ingredient in soapmaking, it's a strong alkaline solution, either sodium hydroxide (for solid soap) or potassium hydroxide (for liquid soap), used to saponify oils and create soap.

Trace: The point during soap making when the soap batter has thickened enough. It's the first sign that an emulsion has stabilized.

Batch: A single quantity of soap mixture made at one time.

Curing: The process of allowing soap to rest and harden over a designated period, typically a few weeks to several months, to improve its quality and longevity.

Melt and Pour (MP): A soap making method that involves melting pre-made soap base, adding colorants, fragrances, and additives, then pouring the mixture into molds.

Cold Process (CP): A traditional soap making method where oils and lye are combined to trigger saponification. The mixture is poured into molds and allowed to cure.

Hot Process (HP): A soap making method similar to cold process, but heat is applied during and after saponification to accelerate the process. HP soaps can be used more quickly after curing.

Superfatting: The intentional addition of extra fats or oils to a soap recipe, ensuring there is some unreacted oil remaining in the final soap for added moisturizing properties.

Essential Oil: A highly concentrated, aromatic oil extracted from plants, often used to add scents to soap.

Fragrance Oil: Synthetic or natural compounds that add fragrance to soap. Fragrance oils come in a wide variety of scents.

Colorant: A substance used to add color to soap, which can be natural (such as herbs, spices, and clays) or synthetic (such as micas and pigments).

Swirling: A technique used to create intricate patterns or designs in soap by blending or layering different colored soap batters.

Layering: A technique where different soap batter is poured in layers of different colors or textures to create visually appealing designs.

Exfoliant: A material added to soap to provide gentle abrasion and aid in the removal of dead skin cells, such as oatmeal, coffee grounds, or poppy seeds.

Curing Rack: A device used to allow air circulation around curing soap, facilitating the drying and hardening process.

pH Level: A measure of the acidity or alkalinity of a substance. Soap should have a pH level around 8-10 for safe use.

Glycerin: A natural byproduct of the saponification process that is moisturizing and helps maintain skin's hydration.

Botanicals: Dried herbs, flowers, or plants added to soap for aesthetic appeal, exfoliation, or skin benefits.

Additives: Ingredients like honey, milk, silk, and other substances added to soap for unique properties.

Curing Time: The duration soap needs to rest and harden after molding before it's ready for use. More gentle soaps need extra curing time.

Gelling: Where soap heats up during saponification, resulting in a translucent or transparent appearance in the center of the soap.

Insulating: Covering newly poured soap with a blanket or towel to trap heat and encourage gelling.

Single Oil Soap: A soap made from a single type of oil, such as olive oil (Castile soap) or coconut oil (Coconut soap).

DOS (Dreaded Orange Spot): A cosmetic issue where soap develops orange-brown spots due to the oxidation of certain oils.

Ingredients to Know and Love

Base Oils/Fats:

Olive Oil: A popular choice amongst soap makers as it's easy to source, cost effective and adds moisturizing properties and produces a gentle, creamy lather.

Coconut Oil: Contributes to a bubbly lather and hardness in soap bars.

Palm Oil (Sustainable): Provides hardness and stability to soap. However, sustainable palm oil can be difficult to source. Always try to find out the origins of palm oil as it may raise concerns about sustainability.

Castor Oil: A tried and tested base oil that creates a rich lather and creates a creamy texture. It also helps to create a protective skin barrier.

Sweet Almond Oil: Great for skin conditions like rashes, psoriasis and eczema, it's high in Vitamins E, A and D. Recommended for dry, flaky skin.

Lye (Sodium Hydroxide or Potassium Hydroxide)

Sodium Hydroxide (NaOH): Also known as lye, is an essential ingredient in soap making.

Potassium Hydroxide (KOH): Used for making liquid soaps.

Additives and Enhancers

Essential Oils: Natural compounds extracted from plants, used for fragrance and potential therapeutic benefits.

Fragrance Oils: Synthetic or natural blends used for scenting soap. Note that these can be an irritant for those with sensitive skin.

Colorants: Substances like micas, pigments, and natural colorants (clays, herbs) to add color.

Botanicals: Dried herbs, flowers, or plant materials added for color, texture, or skin benefits.

Exfoliants: Substances like oatmeal, coffee grounds, and poppy seeds to gently remove dead skin cells. Be sure to find exfoliants that don't have rough edges as it can irritate the skin.

Clays: It can have purifying properties and is great for oily skin.

Milks: Goat milk, cow's milk, or plant-based milks add creaminess and nutrients to soap.

Honey: Adds a sweet scent and helps to create a lather to the soap. It's a natural humectant that has antimicrobial properties. One of its benefits is helping skin retaining its moisture.

Activated Charcoal: Great for oily skin, it provides a deep cleansing effect and absorbs oil and substances that cause inflammation to the skin. The result is a clearer complexion.

Superfatting Agents

Shea Butter: A popular ingredient in soap making, it provides a creamy and moisturising texture to soaps. And it also helps to harden the soap. Ideally for hair conditioners and body soaps designed for dry skin.

Cocoa Butter: A good ingredient if you're looking for something rich with a luxurious feel. Helps soap to harden.

Avocado Oil: Nourishing and rich in vitamins A and E. It's great in conditioners and moisturising body bars.

Liquids

Water: Common liquid used in soap recipes.

Aloe Vera Juice: Adds soothing and moisturizing qualities. It also has an antiseptic effect which is great for people prone to breakouts.

Coconut Milk: Creamy liquid that contributes to a luxurious lather. Coconut milk is known to have anti aging properties and helps to build collagen.

Hardness and Lathering Enhancers

Sodium Lactate: Sodium salt of lactic acid, used to harden soap and improve texture.

Salt: Enhances hardness and lathering of soap.

Preservatives:

Rosemary Extract: A natural antioxidant that helps extend the shelf life of oils in soap.

Chelating Agents

Citric Acid: Used to prevent mineral deposits and maintain clarity in transparent soaps.

pH Adjusters

Borax: Used in small amounts to adjust pH and help with saponification.

Gelling Agents

Sugar: Can help soap batches go through a partial gel phase, resulting in a translucent appearance.

Remember, the ingredients you use can vary based on the type of soap you're making (cold process, hot process, melt and pour, etc.) and your desired outcome. Always follow soap-making recipes and guidelines to ensure safety and successful results.

Adding Scents to Your Soap

Once you've created your base formula, you can start to have some fun with the scent and colours. If you need some inspiration for pairing scents, here are a few to get your creative juices flowing:

1. Lavender and Lemon: A combination of calm and vibrancy. Lavender has a calming scent and is a great balance for the zesty notes of lemon, creating a refreshing and balanced fragrance.

2. Peppermint and Eucalyptus: Fresh and invigorating, this combination awakens your senses.

3. Rosemary and Mint: The herbal and earthy scent of rosemary complements the energizing and crisp fragrance of mint, resulting in a rejuvenating and revitalizing aroma.

4. Vanilla and Coconut: If you want your soap to spell like your next holiday, this is the combination to try. Warm vanilla combined with tropical coconut evokes thoughts of paradise and relaxation, providing a soothing and sweet experience.

5. Citrus Blend: A mix of citrus scents like orange, grapefruit, and lime can a smell that lifts your mood and energise.

6. Sandalwood and Patchouli: Perfect for those who love the smell of natural skincare.

7. Chamomile and Bergamot: A calming and relaxing combination.

8. Jasmine and Neroli: Suited to those who love floral and feminine scents.

9. Oatmeal and Honey: A comforting combination that's soothing on the skin and senses.

10. Spiced Citrus: A mix of cinnamon, clove, and nutmeg with accents of citrus fruits makes a warm and cozy scent.

11. Lemongrass and Ginger: A popular combination in food and in fragrance, the invigorating scent of lemongrass pairs well with the spicy aroma of ginger.

12. Lavender and Rose: The classic elegance of rose combines effortlessly with the soothing and floral notes of lavender, creating a timeless and romantic fragrance.

13. Cedarwood and Bergamot: The woody and grounding essence of cedarwood blends harmoniously with the uplifting and citrusy scent of bergamot, resulting in a balanced and comforting aroma.

14. Mint and Tea Tree: The refreshing and cooling properties of mint complement the invigorating and cleansing qualities of tea tree, offering a revitalizing and clarifying fragrance.

The best soap recipes are a product of trial and error. When in doubt practice and test your scents in small test batches. You'll also need to experiment with different ratios of oil drops needed to achieve your ideal outcome.

Soap Recipes

Luxurious Body Cleansing Bar

The formula on the next page is represented in percentage so that if you would want to substitute any of the ingredients you can do it easily. Ensure that the oil or butter you are using as the substitute will give the same properties as the oil or butter you will be replacing. Be sure to run your new recipe through a lye calculator before attempting to make the soap with the oil substitutes.

Bar Soap Formula

Ingredients %

Coconut Oil 33

Olive Oil 40

Canola Oil 17

Shea Butter 10

Water 33

Ingredient	Measurement
Coconut oil	318.08
Olive oil	385.55
Canola oil	163.86
Shea butter	96.39
Milk powder	23.9
Oatmeal powder	23.9

The soap recipe below was formulated to make 1497.22 g of soap with a superfat of 5%. That's about 8-9 bars.

Ingredient	Measurement
Salt	4.9
Purified or Distilled water	318.08
Lye	137.32
Fragrance	30.14

Step by Step Guide

1. Follow the lye safety steps before measuring out all the ingredients and setting them aside. This is to ensure that you do not forget to add one of the ingredients to the mix. 2. Dissolve the salt in the water. Slowly and carefully add the lye to the water in a well- ventilated area. Gently stir the mixture until the lye fully dissolves and the liquid is relatively clear. Fumes will be given off from the lye water so ensure you are wearing your mask and/or you are mixing it in a well- ventilated area. Set aside to cool. The lye solution can be used what it is 90-100 degrees F.

TIP: ALWAYS add the lye crystals to the water and never the other way around. Adding water to the lye can cause the mixture to bubble out of the container.

3. While the lye solution is cooling, combine all the oils and warm them to 90-100 degrees F. Add the shea butter and allow it to melt. Check that the lye

solution and the melted oils are at or below 90-100 degrees F before proceeding.

TIP: The lye solution and the melted oils don't have to be at the same temperature. They can be *about 10* degrees apart but within the 90-100 degrees Fahrenheit range or below before combining.

4. Add the oatmeal powder to the oils. Burp the stick blender before using it to incorporate the oatmeal powder well, then gently pour the cooled lye solution down the shaft of the stick blender. This helps to reduce the number of bubbles introduced to the mixture.

8. Spray the top of the soap with 99% isopropyl alcohol. Doing so may help to avoid soda ash from forming. Check the soap after 4 to 6 hours to see if it is hard enough to unmold. Because the salt was used, the soap will unmold much faster than 24 hours. Unmold while wearing gloves. TIP: Even if soda ash forms at the end of the cure, a steamer can be used to remove it. Sometimes the ash adds

character to the soap, so removal is the left to the soaper's choice and also the customer's preference

9. Allow the bars of soap to cure in a well-ventilated room for 4-6 weeks. Ensure that they are appropriately spaced for every surface to come in contact with air. During the cure time, water evaporates from the soap making it firmer and longer-lasting in the shower. The soap can be used before the full cure time (2 weeks), but will not last as long. It's best to wait! Happy soaping! TIP: To make the bars have smooth edges, use a potato peeler or a beveller to trim the 12 edges of each bar.

Jojoba and Rosemary Repairing Shampoo Bar

Safety and Best Practices

- Always ensure that you sanitize your equipment & containers before use. You can use 70% isopropyl alcohol to spray on clean equipment the wipe with paper towel.

- Ensure that you maintain a very high level of personal hygiene. Wash your hands or wear gloves before starting & ensure all work surfaces are clean and sanitized.

- Weigh all your ingredients using a digital scale to ensure greatest accuracy.

- If your products have water in them, they will deteriorate very quickly. Ensure that you use a broad-spectrum preservative to protect you and your customers.

- Label your products and include the date they were made and/or when you expect them to expire.

Presentation of Recipe and Formula

Measurements

Both the formula for each product (written in percentages) and a recipe (written in both grams and ounces) have been included in this guide. The formula is given as a weight for weight percentage (w/w%). This is the percentage, by weight, of the ingredients, of the total weight of the mixture.

You will always weigh your ingredients for accuracy and consistency, even if you're using a mixture of liquids and solids.

If you want to create a different amount of product (a different batch size) you'll need to convert the formula into a weight-based measurement, or recipe', so you know how much of each ingredient to use.

These are the steps to take:

- You'll need to first decide on your batch size (how much product you want to make). You can choose an amount in grams or ounces.
- Then turn your percentage-based formula into weight-based measurements (grams or

ounces) depending on your batch size. The calculation you need to do is:

Percentage of ingredient [divided by] 100 [multiplied by] batch size by weight = weight of ingredient

Ingredient Names

I have used the INCI name alongside the commonly used ingredient name. INCI stands for International Nomenclature of Cosmetic Ingredients. This is essentially a universal, worldwide system of naming for cosmetic ingredients, and it's based on the Latin or scientific name.

An important reason for using the INCI name is there may be several different common names used for an ingredient, so by using the INCI name, you can be 100% sure of the actual ingredient that you're supposed to be including. It's also the INCI name that is usually required to be present on a product label.

For example "shea butter" is the common name, but the INCI for shea butter is Butyrospermum Parkii (Shea Butter)

Phase

The formulas are written in phases and the phases are labeled A, B, C, etc. This is to indicate the order in which ingredients are mixed together. Reference is made to phases in the instructions for making the products, to make it really clear how the product is made.

Shampoo Bar Formulation Guide

Jojoba and Rosemary Repairing Shampoo Bar

This is a simple shampoo bar formula that is good for use about two times a week. It has organic ingredients and is suitable for those who are looking for gentle, sulfate-free shampoo.

The purpose of this shampoo is to gently cleanse the hair and scalp of oil and dirt, and to stimulate the scalp to promote healthy growth. It's gentle and cleans the hair and scalp without stripping beneficial sebum from the scalp.

The Sodium Lauryl Sulfoacetate surfactant is mild and has great foaming and cleansing properties.

Vegekeratin was added for its repairing and strengthening properties while the Jojoba oil was added for a natural shine to the hair strands. A natural preservative was added because this product has a water component that was included. As it will also come into contact with water, the preservative was needed to prevent the growth of mold and bacteria and to increase the shelf life of the bars.

The essential oils were added for their fragrance and therapeutic properties to give the bars a lovely, fresh, minty scent. Note that it is recommended to advise everyone to do a skin patch test before using the shampoo.

When combined with water this product should have a pH of 5-5.8.

In keeping with the zero-waste theme, this product can be packaged in biodegradable shrink wrap and stored in metal tins as well.

Jojoba and Rosemary Repairing Shampoo Bar Recipe

Phase	Ingredients	113 g	1360.78 g
A	SLSa	66.67	802.86
A	Rice Flour	15.26	183.71
B	Cocobetaine	7.91	95.25
B	Water	4.52	54.43
B	Jojoba Oil	9.61	115.67
B	Mixed Tocopherol 50	1.70	20.41
B	Leucidal Liquid	2.26	27.22
B	Rosemary EO	0.85	10.21
B	Sweet Orange EO	0.85	10.21
B	Vegekeratin	3.39	40.82

Manufacturing Instructions

1. Put on a mask or a respirator to protect your airways from the light particles of the ingredients in phase A. Combine all phase A ingredients in a large container. Stir to incorporate well.

2. Add the phase B ingredients to the container with the phase A ingredients and stir well. You will need to use your hands to ensure the mixture is combined properly. It is recommended that you use gloves for this process while you use your hands to mix.

When combined you can use your hands to shape the product or press it into molds. Allow the shampoo bars to set for 2-3 days week before packaging. It is recommended to let them continue to sit for a full week to make them last longer.

Repair and Rejuvenate Conditioner Bar

Conditioner Bar Formulation Guide

Recommended Suppliers

USA and Canada

www.lotioncrafter.com

www.formulatorsampleshop.com

www.theherbarie.com

www.makingcosmetics.com

www.wholesalesuppliesplus.com

www.mountainroseherbs.com

www.amazon.com

Europe

www.aroma-zone.com (France)

www.aliacura.de (Germany)

www.glamourcosmetics.it (Italy)

Jojoba and Rosemary Conditioner Bar

This is a simple, yet effective, conditioner bar formula that can be used as a wash-off or a leave-in product. It is suitable for use after each shampooing and has both natural and naturally derived ingredients in the formula.

The purpose of this conditioner bar is to improve the feel and appearance of the hair but also to help repair damage done to the hair. It has a soothing minty-orange scent that can be uplifting to the end user but also targets scalp issues to stimulate the hair follicles and promote healthy growth.

It has BTMS which is known as a mild and excellent conditioning agent with wonderful detangling properties to condition the hair. It also helps to improve wet comb and leaves the hair with a natural shine and spring. Hydrolyzed Jojoba protein was included to help with hair repair. It works to achieve this by forming a film around each hair strand to help them retain moisture.

Plant oils and shea butter were included to offer natural slip and shine to the product as well as give it a unique marketing story.

A naturally derived preservative was included for safety to prevent bacterial growth because the product will be used in water. Rosemary essential oil and sweet orange essential oil were included for their smell but also to improve scalp conditions and stimulate hair growth respectively.

This product can be packaged using biodegradable shrink wrap and metal tins to add a zero-waste theme to the marketing story.

Jojoba and Rosemary Conditioner Bar Formula

Phase	Ingredients	INCI	Supplier	w/w %
A	BTMS MB	Behentrimonium Methosulfate (and) Cetearyl Alcohol	www.lotioncrafter.com	36

A	Cetyl Alcohol	Cetyl Alcohol	www.lotioncrafter.com	10
A	Stearic Acid	Stearic Acid	www.lotioncrafter.com	26
A	Avocado Oil	Persea Gratissima (Avocado) Fruit Oil	www.lotioncrafter.com	2
A	Jojoba Oil	Simmondsia chinensis (Jojoba) Seed Oil	www.lotioncrafter.com	3
A	Castor Oil	Ricinus Communis (Castor) Seed Oil	www.lotioncrafter.com	2
A	Shea Butter	Butyrospermum Parkii (Shea Butter)	www.lotioncrafter.com	3
B	Glycerin	Glycerin	www.lotioncrafter.com	5

B	Hydrolyzed Jojoba Protein	Hydrolyzed Jojoba Protein, Water, Phenoxyethanol, Potassium Sorbate	www.makingcosmetics.com	5
C	Mixed Tocopherol 50	Tocopherol	www.lotioncrafter.com	1.5
C	Rosemary EO	Rosmarinus officinalis	www.mountainroseherbs.com	0.075
C	Sweet Orange EO	Citrus sinensis	www.mountainroseherbs.com	0.75
D	PhytoCide Elderberry OS	Sambucus nigra Fruit Extract	www.formulatorsampleshop.com	5

Jojoba and Rosemary Conditioner Bar Recipe

Phase	Ingredients	113 g (test batch)	1360.78 g (full batch)
A	BTMS MB	40.68	489.88
A	Cetyl Alcohol	11.30	136.08
A	Stearic Acid	29.38	353.80
A	Avocado Oil	2.26	27.22
A	Jojoba Oil	3.39	40.82
A	Castor Oil	2.26	27.22
A	Shea Butter	3.39	40.82
B	Glycerin	5.65	68.04
B	Hydrolyzed Jojoba Protein	5.65	68.04
C	Mixed Tocopherol 50	1.70	20.41
C	Rosemary EO	0.08	1.02
C	Sweet Orange EO	0.85	10.21
D	PhytoCide Elderberry OS	5.65	68.04

Manufacturing Instructions

3. Combine all phase A ingredients in a heat-safe container. Place the heat safe container with all the ingredients in a water bath until they have melted.
4. While phase A is melting, combine phase B in a separate heat-safe container and set aside.
5. Do the same thing with phase C and set aside.
6. When phase A has melted allow it to cool to 149-158 degrees F before incorporating phase B. Stir until fully incorporated.
7. Add phase C and D to the mixture and stir thoroughly.

Pour into molds and allow to set overnight until solid.

Recommended Suppliers

USA and Canada

www.lotioncrafter.com

www.formulatorsampleshop.com

www.theherbarie.com

www.makingcosmetics.com

www.wholesalesuppliesplus.com

www.mountainroseherbs.com

www.amazon.com

Europe

www.aroma-zone.com (France)

www.aliacura.de (Germany)

www.glamourcosmetics.it (Italy)

Testing Your Soaps

Once you've created your soaps, you'll need to test them for their efficacy and safety. If you intend to sell them for profit, you may also want to consider product and liability insurance. Requirements for doing so are different for each country. Ensure you check the regulations before they sell like hot cakes!

Here's a guide on how to effectively test your soaps and prioritize safety throughout the process:

1. Skin Patch Test

Before using a new soap, do a skin patch test. To do so, use the soap on a small part of your skin, like your forearm. Wait for 24 hours to see if you skin reacts to it.

2. pH Testing

pH testing is a tried and tested way to test a product's safety. A safe pH range for the skin is around 4.75-5.75. Anything too low or too high would irritate the skin. You can purchase pH testing strips to measure your soap's pH level.

3. Offer samples to test a variety of Skin Types

Test your soap on different skin types to gather a broader understanding of how it performs for various individuals.

Safety First

Safety comes first when you're soap making. As you'll be working with different ingredients and chemicals, you'll need to create a safe workspace.

Safety Gear

Always wear appropriate safety gear when handling lye and other chemicals. Safety goggles, gloves, and close toed shoes are a must. Have a first aid kit on hand and ensure it's well stocked.

Ventilation

Soap making can produce fumes that may be unsafe and uncomfortable. Work in a well-ventilated area to prevent inhaling fumes. If working indoors, use fans or open windows to ensure proper air circulation.

Proper Mixing

Mix lye into water (not water into lye) to prevent splattering. Mix lye solution and oils thoroughly to ensure complete saponification.

Test the Lye Solution

When mixing lye, ensure the lye solution is clear and free from undissolved lye crystals. Allow it to cool to the desired temperature before adding to oils.

Avoid Contamination

Keep your workspace clean and free from potential contaminants. Sterilize equipment and utensils before use.

Remember, safety is paramount when making soap. Always follow established guidelines and recommendations to ensure a safe and enjoyable soap-making experience.

Your Soap Making Start Up Guide

Now that we've covered the soap making side, let's get down to business. If you love soap making and want to turn your passion into profit, this section was designed for you. But if you're only interested in the business side of things, we've got you covered too. You don't need to be great at soap making to create a thriving soap business. In the following chapters we will cover how you can build a business from scratch.

Why start a soap making business

With more consumers becoming conscious about the use of plastic in skincare, many are exploring alternative body and skincare solutions that promote zero waste. While the market continues to innovate its zero waste beauty products, there remains a lot of space for independent makers to run a profitable business. Other than setting your own work hours, another reason to start a soap making business is that with the right branding and packaging, you can price your soaps to gain a higher margin. With online and offline sales channels available, there are many ways to sell your soaps.

Aside from a more conscious customer, consider these factors as you explore the profit potential of soap making:

Premium Pricing: Handcrafted soap can command premium prices due to its artisanal nature and high-quality ingredients. This allows you to earn higher profit margins compared to traditional commodity products.

Repeat Business: A satisfied customer is a loyal customer. When you create soap that delivers exceptional results and a delightful experience, you foster customer loyalty and repeat business, contributing to sustained revenue.

Diverse Revenue Streams: As your business evolves, you can diversify your product offerings, from specialty soap bars to complementary items like bath bombs, lotions, and candles, expanding your revenue streams.

Growing Online Marketplaces: Don't fancy selling at local markets? No worries. With social media and platforms like Etsy, it's easy to reach customers from all around the world.

How much can you earn make selling soaps

Soap makers can earn a part time to full time income depending on the quality of their products, branding and marketing strategy. With the right positioning and brand story, you can price your products higher than the competition. Let's have a look at an example:

Let's say it takes about $1.50 to produce a bar of soap (not including your time). If you position your soap as a premium product highlighting its efficacy and ingredients, you could price your products 3-7x the cost.

In our scenario, we will price our soap at $8. That's about $6.50 profit on each bar. Many customers typically buy more than one bar. If they purchase 3 bars of soap in a bundle deal for $20, you'd make a profit of $15.50 per sale.

Now if you're open to wholesale orders, you can price your soap for $4 each. But each order requires a MOQ (minimum order quantity) of 50 bars. If a business purchased 50 bars, you'd make a $200 sale. With the cost price being $75, you'd make a profit of $125.

Where to begin

Building a business doesn't need to be overwhelming. We've broken the process up into several steps. Set a deadline for yourself and just get started. Too often people tend to overthink, and it stops them from taking action. The sooner you start, the faster you'll launch your beautiful products to people who need them.

Many people start a business by creating a product they personally love but just because you love something, it doesn't necessarily mean there will be a market for it. If you're moving away from soap making as a hobby into a business, you'll need to carve out an audience. By finding your people, you'll be able to get a better direction for your packaging, brand positioning and pricing.

For example, people who love to shop at the local farmer's market may be different from those who shop at high end department stores. Let's say your target audience is someone who shops at Neiman Marcus or a similar luxury retailer. Use the following prompts to identify your ideal people to market to.

Questions to identify your ideal audience

1. What does your ideal audience care about? e.g. the environment, feeling comfortable, a healthy lifestyle…

2. How does your audience spend their money? e.g. Takeaway and nice dinners, fast fashion, healthy nutritious food, personal trainers…etc.

3. What industry does your audience tend to work in?

4. What hobbies do they have?

5. What motivates them to make a purchase? e.g. price, comfort, promise to deliver results, influencers…etc.

Create a unique selling proposition

Once you've identified your ideal audience, you'll want to create an offering that suits their needs and wants. This includes your product offering, your branding and messaging.

To create your unique selling proposition, start by looking at what's available in the market. And don't just limit your search to products in your category e.g. body care. Look to industries like fashion, homewares or home cleaning products for inspiration. That'll help you develop a brand personality that's truly unique.

Next up, have a look at your competitors. What products are they offering? This is where you can really stand out. There are many shampoo and conditioner bars emerging from natural health stores but very few have tapped into zero waste skincare. Think about your beauty cabinet and consider what could be transformed into bar form e.g. facial oil bar, facial bar serum, eye cream bar…etc.

Crafting Your Identity: Choosing the Perfect Business Name

Your business name is more than a label; it's the essence of your brand. Though you can always change it later, it's best to get it right from the start. Consider the following:

Reflect Your Brand: Your business name should reflect the essence of your soap making business. Consider the emotions, values, and characteristics you want your brand to convey.

Memorable and Unique: Select a name that is easy to remember and stands out in the minds of customers.

Domain Availability: Ensure that the domain name and social media handles for your business website are available.

Legal Considerations: Check for trademark availability and register your business name to protect it legally.

Cultural Sensitivity: Research cultural and linguistic nuances to avoid unintentional misunderstandings or misinterpretations.

Crafting a Solid Business Plan

Starting a business of any kind can be overwhelming but if you create a solid business plan, you'll always have a direction and a goal to work towards. Let's dive in a create one for you budding business.

The foundations of a business plan

Business Overview: This is a brief description of your soap making business, your brand, your product offering, and unique selling proposition (we'll get into this later one).

Executive Summary: Summarize the key points of your business plan, here's where I'd highlight your goals and milestones you'd like to achieve e.g. make $10k a month in sales and have your range distributed in department stores.

Market Analysis: Highlights the market research you've done to understand your target audience, competition, and industry trends.

Defining Your Mission, Vision, and Values

Mission Statement: What problem are you trying to solve for your customers?

Vision Statement: How do you want to achieve your goals? What does the end result look like?

Values and Ethics: Outline the values that underpin your business, emphasizing integrity, sustainability, and social responsibility.

Mapping Out Financial Projections and Growth Strategies

Financial Projections: Provide a detailed overview of your soap making business's financial forecast. Include projected revenue, expenses, and profit margins over a specific period (e.g., 1-3 years).

Budget Allocation: Break down your budget allocation for various business components, such as production, marketing, operations, and growth initiatives.

Growth Strategies: Outline strategies for expanding your soap making business, whether through market diversification, geographical expansion, or the introduction of new product lines.

Risk Assessment: Identify potential risks and challenges that your business may face, along with contingency plans to mitigate these risks and ensure continuity.

Milestones and Metrics: Set measurable milestones and key performance indicators (KPIs) that will serve as benchmarks to track your progress and evaluate the success of your business plan.

A well-crafted business plan is more than a document; it's a roadmap that empowers you to navigate the complex terrain of entrepreneurship with confidence and clarity. As you meticulously outline your mission, vision, and financial projections, you're not just planning for the present but laying the groundwork for a soap making business that thrives and endures.

Develop a budget

Before you deep dive into branding, marketing and procurement, it's best to set a budget. In doing so, you'll learn how much capital you'll need to get started and how long it might take you to break even. It'll also be a helpful guide for negotiating with your suppliers. Here are a few things you'll want to consider when creating your budget.

Start-Up Costs: Calculate the initial investment required for equipment, ingredients, packaging, and marketing. Consider both one-time expenses and ongoing operational costs.

Financial Projections: Create a detailed financial forecast that estimates your revenue, expenses, and profit margins. This projection will guide your decision-making and provide a clear overview of your business's financial health.

Pricing Strategy: Determine the pricing structure for your soap products. Consider factors such as material costs, labour, overhead, and desired profit margin. Ensure that your pricing is competitive while reflecting the quality and value you offer.

Working Capital: Maintain a cushion of working capital to cover day-to-day expenses, unexpected costs, and to facilitate growth opportunities.

Cash Flow Management: Monitor your cash flow to ensure that you have enough liquidity to cover expenses and investments. Cash flow management is crucial for the smooth operation of your business.

If you're new to spreadsheets, and want a simple solution, email me at iona@prettypickleshop.com and I'll send you a few helpful resources.

Source your product

If soap making isn't aligned with your personal schedule, you can still build a thriving business. A common way to source your ideal range without making it yourself is through white labelling. With white labelling, you can work with manufacturers who create products without a label. You can purchase the product in bulk and put your own branding and packaging on it.

If you prefer to create your own formulations, you can also work with a cosmetic chemist or manufacturer to create and produce your own formulation. If you're on a budget, you'll need to be mindful of MOQs (minimum order quantity). Smaller manufacturers tend to have less MOQs (10-20 products as a minimum order) and you might want to start with those until you have a proof of concept and your products are making consistent sales.

Identify your selling channels

Once you've built a brand and have a range of products you're happy with, it's time to start exploring your sales channels. When it comes to selling, always opt for multiple revenue streams, in case one falls through. This will ensure you always have a sustainable income. Here are a mix of online and offline channels to consider.

Online Marketplaces: Platforms like Etsy, Amazon Handmade are all designed for makers. Not only are they easy to use, they also generate traffic to your shop. You'll have to pay fees to be a seller but they would be much less than your typical marketing and advertising costs. Some makers go straight to setting up their own e-commerce store but I wouldn't advise unless you have an existing following or have the budget to drive traffic to your website.

Farmers Markets: Local markets are a great way to meet locals and promote your brand. They're also a good way to sell to those who are hesitant to shop online.

Retail Partnerships: Collaborate with local boutiques, gift shops, or health stores to stock your soap products on their shelves, expanding your reach to a broader audience.

Social Media and Influencer Collaborations: If you can find micro influencers (those with an audience under 10k), you can most likely gift them product in exchange for a social media mention. Influencer collaborations are a great way to build a following.

Positioning and Branding Your Soap Business

Your soap business is about crafting an experience that resonates with your target audience. Use the following in your story telling.

Origin Story: Share the journey that led you to the world of soap making. Highlight personal anecdotes, challenges you overcame, and the inspiration behind your creations.

Ingredients and Process: Educate your audience about the carefully selected ingredients and meticulous processes that go into each soap bar, emphasizing quality and craftsmanship. It doesn't matter if you haven't created the soap yourself. With the help of your manufacturer, you can craft a compelling story.

Values and Mission: Articulate your business's core values, ethical commitments, and the positive impact you aspire to create in the lives of your customers. It could be a message about zero waste or just knowing where your products come from.

Visual Identity Matters: Designing a Compelling Logo and Brand Aesthetics

Logo Design: Craft a visually appealing and memorable logo. It doesn't need to be an expensive task. You can easily purchase a template from Etsy or hire a designer from Fivver to create one for you.

Color Palette and Typography: Choose a color palette and typography that evoke emotions and resonate with your brand's character. If you need inspiration, Pinterest and Canva are a great place to start.

Photography and Visual Content: Invest in high-quality product photography and visual content that showcase your soap products in an alluring and aspirational light.

From Small to Big: Scaling Your Soap Business

Production Expansion: Invest in larger equipment and workspaces to increase production capacity, ensuring that your supply keeps up with growing demand.

Outsourcing: Collaborate with other soap makers or manufacturers to outsource certain stages of production while maintaining your unique formulation and quality standards.

Diversification: Expand your product offering by introducing complementary items such as body scrubs, bath bombs, or skincare accessories, appealing to a broader customer base.

Streamlining Operations: Automating Processes and Optimizing Efficiency

Inventory Management: Implement inventory tracking systems to monitor stock levels, anticipate demand, and prevent stockouts or overstocking.

Order Fulfillment: Streamline order processing, packaging, and shipping procedures to ensure timely and accurate delivery to customers.

Technology Integration: Utilize software solutions for bookkeeping, customer relationship management (CRM), and e-commerce platforms to streamline administrative tasks.

Expanding Your Product Line: Introducing New Soap Variations and Related Products

Market Research: Identify emerging trends and customer preferences to develop innovative soap variations that cater to evolving demands.

Limited Editions: Create limited-edition soap collections for special occasions, seasons, or collaborations to generate excitement and urgency among your customer base.

Value-Added Products: Introduce related products like soap dishes, accessories, or gift sets that enhance the overall customer experience and offer additional value.

When Time is of the Essence: Wholesale and White Labelling

In the fast-paced world of soap making business, there are moments when seizing opportunities swiftly becomes paramount. This chapter delves into two strategic avenues that allow you to broaden your business horizons efficiently: wholesale and white labelling. These paths not only expand your market reach but also facilitate collaboration and growth.

Exploring the World of Wholesale: Selling Your Products in Bulk to Retailers

Benefits of Wholesale: Wholesale offers the potential for larger sales volumes and broader exposure as your soap products reach a network of retailers. It can provide a stable and consistent revenue stream.

Retailer Relationships: Cultivate relationships with retailers who share your brand values and target audience. Nurture open communication, reliability, and professionalism to foster long-term partnerships.

Pricing Considerations: Develop a competitive yet profitable pricing structure for your wholesale products. Factor in costs, profit margins, and the retailer's pricing strategy.

Packaging and Presentation: Ensure your soap products are presented attractively, reflecting your brand identity and maintaining consistency in quality and appearance.

White Labelling: Partnering with Established Brands to Put Your Soap Creations on the Map

Defining White Labelling: White labelling involves creating soap products for other brands, allowing you to leverage their existing customer base and distribution channels.

Brand Collaboration: Collaborate with established brands that align with your values and offer mutual benefits. White labelling can extend your reach while enhancing the partner brand's product range.

Quality Assurance: Maintain the same level of quality and craftsmanship as you do for your own brand. Consistency is vital to uphold your reputation and meet partner brand expectations.

Branding Sensitivity: Respect the partner brand's image and guidelines while infusing your unique touch. Balance your creativity with adhering to the established brand's identity.

Now that you know the basics, get started

You can plan, plan and plan but the best way to start a business is just to dive in a do something about it. Remember that success is not a linear path. Just like any other business owner, you'll go through your highs and lows, your busy and slow seasons. With careful planning and a will to succeed, you've got this!

Notes

Notes

Notes

www.ingramcontent.com/pod-product-compliance
Lightning Source LLC
Chambersburg PA
CBHW010707020526
44107CB00082B/2709